The Tractor

by Alison Hawes

illustrated by Esther Pérez-Cuadrado

Institute of Education

We can see the farm.

We can see the goats.

We can see the cows.

7

We can see the chickens.

We can see the rain.

10

We can see the mud.

We can see the tractor!

Tractor ● Alison Hawes

Teaching notes written by Sue Bodman and Glen Franklin

Using this book

Developing reading comprehension

The family have arrived for a visit to the farm.
The sentence structure is repeated, with the events communicated by the illustrations. Punctuation is changed to an exclamation mark on the last page to support meaning.

Grammar and sentence structure

- Text is well-spaced to support the development of one-to-one correspondence.

- One line of text uses high frequency words and a change to the noun on each page. This is supported by clear illustrations and the noun appearing as the last word of each sentence.

- In contexts where children are learning English as an additional language, support by rehearsing the sentence structure orally before introducing the book.

Word meaning and spelling

- Use letter information to check vocabulary choice ('farm', 'goats', 'cows', ' chickens', 'rain' 'mud', 'tractor').

- Reinforce recognition of frequently occurring words 'We can see the ...'.

Curriculum links

Geography – Explore the range of food people get from farms: crops, dairy and meat, in the school's locality.

Science and Maths – Set up a mud kitchen experiment and see what happens to earth and sand when water is added.

Learning outcomes

Children can:

- understand that print carries meaning and is read from left to right

- use initial letter information to check understanding of picture information

- track one line of simple repetitive text.

A guided reading lesson

Book introduction

Give a book to each child and read the title. Discuss with the children what a tractor is, and why it is used on farms. Ask them to say 'tractor' aloud and listen for the first sound /t/. Write the letter explaining that /t/ can be written in lower case and upper case to prepare the children for the lower case form in the book.

Orientation

Give a brief orientation to the text: *The family are visiting the farm. They will have an exciting day and see lots of animals.*

Preparation

Page 2: Say: *The children say 'We can see the farm.'* Read the text slowly enough for the children to match carefully as you read. Praise, repeat and support if necessary.

Say: *Make sure you point carefully when you read.*

Page 4: Support the change of the noun. Say: *On this page, she says 'We can see the goats.' Can you see the word that says 'goats'? Use the letters to find it; 'goats'. Yes, that's right. I can hear /g/ at the beginning. This letter helps me know the word says 'goats'. Now let's read it together – 'We can see the goats'.* Check that the children are pointing to each word as they read.